TITANIC
COLORING BOOK FOR KIDS
30 Coloring Activities to Learn about the *Titanic*

Illustrations by Bookworks.in

callisto
publishing
an imprint of Sourcebooks

Copyright © 2022 by Callisto Publishing LLC
Cover and internal design © 2022 by Callisto Publishing LLC
Illustrations © 2022 Bookworks.in
Interior and Cover Designer: Irene Vandervoort
Art Producer: Megan Baggott
Editor: Julie Haverkate
Production Editor: Cassie Gitkin
Production Manager: Martin Worthington

Published by Callisto Publishing LLC C/O Sourcebooks LLC
P.O. Box 4410, Naperville, Illinois 60567-4410
(630) 961-3900
callistopublishing.com

This product conforms to all applicable CPSC and CPSIA standards.

Source of Production: P.A. Hutchinson Company
Date of Production: December 2023
Run Number: 5037327

Printed and bound in the United States of America
PAH 2

INTRODUCTION

Hello, and welcome to this coloring book! The *Titanic* was one of the most famous ships of its time. Tragically, after only a few days at sea, the *Titanic* sank to the bottom of the Atlantic Ocean after striking an iceberg in the night. Even though it's been sitting on the ocean floor for more than one hundred years, the *Titanic*'s history still captivates us.

This coloring book will answer all your curious questions and more. You'll learn where exactly the *Titanic* set sail, what its deck floors were made of, and what life was like for people aboard, from first- to third-class passengers and the crew. Did you know the *Titanic* had a twin ship? Or that there was a swimming pool on board?

On each page, you will find a unique image of the *Titanic*'s journey waiting to be brought to life with your coloring, plus a fun fact about its voyage.

Before you start, grab your crayons, markers, or colored pencils. Come aboard now to discover some of the most extraordinary facts about the unforgettable *Titanic*...

The *Titanic* was more than 882 feet long—as long as 25 full-size
school buses end to end.

More than three thousand people spent three years building the *Titanic*.

The *Titanic* and its twin ship, the *Olympic*, were built side by side.

The *Titanic* left Belfast, Ireland, on April 2, 1912, and headed to Southampton, England, to prepare for its first trip—its maiden voyage.

On April 10, 1912, the *Titanic* set sail for its very first trip
across the Atlantic Ocean.

One hundred thousand people cheered when the ship sailed away
from Southampton, England.

The *Titanic* picked up passengers in Southampton, England; Cherbourg, France; and Queenstown, Ireland. It was meant to steam on to New York City.

Only three of the *Titanic*'s four funnels were real smokestacks.

Ten passenger decks were fashioned from the finest pine flooring.

The forward Grand Staircase was one of the *Titanic*'s
most beautiful interior creations.

Dinner in first class included ten courses. Finishing all ten plates
of food could take up to four hours.

The third-class dining room had long, narrow tables side by side.
Coat hooks for hats and jackets lined the walls.

First-class ticket holders could read in the library.

Men and women weren't allowed to swim in the heated
saltwater pool at the same time.

The Turkish Bath was a series of hot rooms, followed by
"shampooing rooms" for massages, a steam room, and an electric bath.

The *Titanic*'s first-class gymnasium had a mechanical horse
and a mechanical camel.

A first-class cabin on the *Titanic* would cost $3,500 today.

The *Titanic*'s parlor staterooms were expensive but luxurious.

A wireless radio system sent out messages in Morse code—
one letter at a time in a code of dots and dashes.

The *Titanic*'s lookouts were in the crow's nest, fifty feet above the deck.
It was their job to search the sea for danger.

Late in the evening on April 14, the lookouts spotted a large shadow
in the water and saw the *Titanic* was headed straight for it.

At 11:40 p.m. on April 14, the *Titanic* hit a mountain
of floating ice called an iceberg.

The side of the *Titanic* crashed against the iceberg. Its
hull was torn. Rivets popped and opened holes.

The captain gave the order: Wake the passengers and load them
into the lifeboats.

The *Titanic* had only twenty lifeboats for a total of 1,178 seats.
More than a thousand people would be left behind.

The *Titanic* orchestra played calming music until the very end.

In just two hours and forty minutes, the *Titanic* had sunk.

It's estimated that around 712 people survived the wreck.

For many years, the location of the *Titanic* was unknown. In 1985, Dr. Robert Ballard found the wreck of the *Titanic*.

The battered bow of the *Titanic*'s hull was found
buried 60 feet beneath the ocean floor.